Stronger Together

Studies in a Covenant for Mission

In 2021 Churches Together in Evesham & District (CTED) developed and approved a Covenant for Mission. This is printed in full below. The Covenant brings into focus the reason for our existence as one body in Christ serving God's mission together in the Vale of Evesham. It is part of the process of growing together in Christ through common prayer and worship, mutual listening, understanding, action and love, that we may be renewed together for mission

This booklet consists of seven sessions which can be used in a wide variety of ways, among which may be:
- a series of sermons or
- a series of sermons followed by discussion at the time or on a later occasion or
- a series of study groups or
- whatever arrangement is best in your context.

The studies should preferably be used ecumenically, or by individual congregations or groups of churches.

Each unit of material is constructed in such a way as to enable it to be adapted to the context in which it is used. The sessions differ from one another in detail but the overall pattern is:

- A statement of the theme taken from the Covenant for Mission.
- A prayer that unites all who use the studies.
- A Bible reading or readings.
- Some notes that could be used in a sermon or as an introduction to a study group.
- Discussion starters based on the biblical passage(s) and the relevant section of the Covenant.
- Some suggestions for prayer, which could be used in public worship or a study group.

The Appendix consists of a selection of ideas or quotations relevant to each chapter that a preacher or study group leader may find helpful, inspiring or challenging.

We wish you God's blessing as you use what we offer.

Mark Binney
John Darby
Christine Dodd
Stephen Mizzi
Robert Paterson - convenor & editor
Edward Pillar
Chris Sheehan
Andy Smith
Andrew Spurr

Stronger Together

Studies in
A Covenant for Mission

CHURCHES
TOGETHER
in Evesham & District

© Copyright
Churches Together in Evesham and District 2022

ISBN
978-1-387-88892-4

Bible translations are

The New Revised Standard Version (NRSV)

© 1989 Division of Christian Education of
National Council of Churches of Christ in the USA
Anglicised version published in London by Collins Publishers

and

The Revised English Bible (REB)

© Oxford and Cambridge University Press 1989

Both are the product of ecumenical collaboration

Cover photo by krakenimages on Unsplash

Other images by
Simon Brown, Lucas Becker, Aaron Burden, Matt Collamer, Zac Durant, Nick Fewings, Alex Forester, Juri Gianfrancesco, Ia Huh, Helena Lopes, Tim Marshall, Adrian Moise, MRJN Photography, Ben Richards, Larm Rmah, Sunguk Kim, Ashin K Suresh, Rohit Tandon and Jon Tyson

Contents

	Page
Foreword	4
A Covenant for Mission	6
Bright ideas to share	9
1 The love of God	12
2 Making Jesus Christ known	20
3 Serving human need	26
4 Being one body	32
5 Exercising God's gifts	40
6 Stronger together	46
7 The way forward	52
Appendix of additional material	59

A Covenant for Mission

The love of God for humanity recalls Christians to the covenant relationship of grace and mercy in which God holds the Church and the world.

As churches that confess their faith in one God, Father, Son and Holy Spirit, and conscious of the special relationship with one another in Christ,

- we give thanks for all we have in common;
- we acknowledge the richness of our diversity;
- we are ashamed of the continuing consequences of division;
- we share our understanding of the obedience to which we are called.

Making Jesus Christ known

1. **a** We recognise in one another the same faith in Jesus Christ revealed in the Holy Scriptures, which the creeds of the ancient Church and other historic confessions seek to safeguard. We recognise in one another the same desire to hold this faith and proclaim the gospel in all its fullness.

   b We intend so to act, speak and serve together in obedience to our Lord that the gospel of Jesus might be made known to others through the witness of our words, our lives and our faithfulness to Christ.

Serving human need

2. **a** We recognise in one another a shared awareness of God's call to serve his gracious purpose for all humanity.

   b We intend to work together for the freedom to flourish for all humanity, for justice and peace, for the healing of creation, and for the spiritual well-being of all.

Being one body

3. a We recognise one another as members of the Church of Jesus Christ, sharing in the unity of the Holy Spirit and committed to work for the coming of his Kingdom.

  b We intend by the help of the Spirit to overcome those divisions which impede God's mission, obscure the gospel, and impair our witness. We intend to manifest our unity in Christ, that the world may believe.

Exercising God's gifts

4. a We recognise in one another the same call to every believer to share in the service of the church to the world, just as Christ lived among us as a servant.

  b We intend to seek those forms of common life which will enable all Christians to use the gifts bestowed on them in the service of God.

Stronger together

5. a We recognise in our congregational lives and patterns of worship, marks of love, joy, peace and holiness which are among the fruits of the Spirit.

  b We intend to listen to one another and to appreciate the life and treasures of our various traditions, in order that the riches entrusted to us in separation may build up the whole Church of Christ.

In faithfulness to the Word of God we believe that God will guide his Church into ways of truth and peace, correcting and healing, strengthening and renewing according to the mind of Christ. We approach the future with openness to the Holy Spirit.

We therefore urge the people of all our churches to love one another in the Holy Spirit as God loves the world, and to take every opportunity to grow together in Christ through common prayer and worship, mutual listening, understanding, action and love, that we may be renewed together for mission.

We are committed before God and with one another to the Covenant for Mission: to work and pray in common obedience to our Lord Jesus Christ, that by the power of the Holy Spirit we may serve together in Evesham and District for the coming of the Kingdom and to the glory of God the Father.

*The Covenant was signed by church leaders
at a united service on 28 November, Advent Sunday, 2021*

What is Churches Together in Evesham and District?

CTED [c-ted], as its name suggests, is the whole family of Christian communities in the town of Evesham and the surrounding villages.

It is led by an Enabling Group, consisting of two representatives appointed by each member church who meet several times a year to support the common life of the churches.

CTED is associated with a number of independent agencies and groups, such as Caring Hands and Street Pastors.

Bright ideas to share

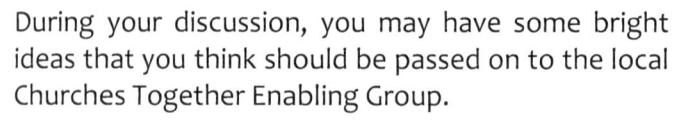

During your discussion, you may have some bright ideas that you think should be passed on to the local Churches Together Enabling Group.

Please note them here.

---

1 The love of God

---

2 Making Jesus Christ known

---

3 Serving human need

---

4 Being one body

5 Exercising God's gifts

6 Stronger together

7 The way forward

Your comments on the course itself will also be welcome.

Thank you for participating and for your responses.

1 The love of God

Our opening Covenant commitment to God and one another

The love of God for humanity recalls Christians to the covenant relationship of grace and mercy in which God holds the Church and the world.

As churches that confess their faith in one God, Father, Son and Holy Spirit, and conscious of the special relationship with one another in Christ,

- we give thanks for all we have in common;
- we acknowledge the richness of our diversity;
- we are ashamed of the continuing consequences of division;
- we share our understanding of the obedience to which we are called.

The Covenant Prayer

Loving Lord God,
we give you thanks for calling us together.
Guide us today
that in common obedience to our Lord Jesus Christ
and by the power of your Holy Spirit
we may learn together to serve you more faithfully
and search for the coming of your kingdom.
Amen.

Bible readings

1 John 4. 7-12 (REB)

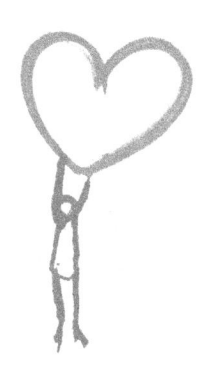

My dear friends, let us love one another, because the source of love is God. Everyone who loves is a child of God and knows God, [8] but the unloving know nothing of God, for God is love. [9] This is how he showed his love among us: he sent his only Son into the world that we might have life through him. ¹⁰ This is what love really is: not that we have loved God, but that he loved us and sent his Son as a sacrifice to atone for our sins. ¹¹ If God thus loved us, my dear friends, we also must love one another. ¹² God has never been seen by anyone, but if we love one another, he himself dwells in us; his love is brought to perfection within us.

John 13. 1-17, 34 (REB)

It was before the Passover festival, and Jesus knew that his hour had come and that he must leave this world and go to the Father. He had always loved his own who were in the world, and he loved them to the end.
² The devil had already put it into the mind of Judas son of Simon Iscariot to betray him. During supper, ³ Jesus, well aware that the Father had entrusted everything to him, and that he had come from God and was going back to God, ⁴ rose from the supper table, took off his outer garment and, taking a towel, tied it round him. ⁵ Then he poured water into a basin, and began to wash his disciples' feet and to wipe them with the towel.
⁶ When he came to Simon Peter, Peter said to him, 'You, Lord, washing my feet?' ⁷ Jesus replied, 'You do not understand now what I am doing, but one day you will.' ⁸ Peter said, 'I will never let you wash my feet.' 'If I do not wash you,' Jesus replied, 'you have no part with me.' ⁹ 'Then, Lord,' said Simon Peter, 'not my feet only; wash my hands and head as well!'
¹⁰ Jesus said to him, 'Anyone who has bathed needs no further washing; he is clean all over; and you are clean, though not every one of you.' ¹¹ He added the words 'not every one of you' because he knew who was going to betray him.
¹² After washing their feet he put on his garment and sat down again. 'Do you understand what I have done for you?' he asked. ¹³ 'You call me Teacher and Lord, and rightly so, for that is what I am. ¹⁴ Then if I, your Lord and Teacher, have washed your feet, you also ought to wash one another's feet. ¹⁵ I have set you an example: you are to do as I have done for you. ¹⁶ In very truth I tell you, a servant is not greater than his master, nor a

messenger than the one who sent him. ¹⁷ *If you know this, happy are you if you act upon it. ...*
³⁴ *I give you a new commandment: love one another; as I have loved you, so you are to love one another.*

Sermon outline / Introduction

Our commitment to one another as Churches rests on the foundation of the love of God.

The Bible passage from 1 John reminds us that God is love. That's a powerful and profound statement: 'God is love'.

When the Apostle John asserts that God is love he is reflecting the deep well of occasions in the Old Testament where we read that God is love.

When God reveals himself to Moses *(see Exodus 34)* God's own self-description is, '"The LORD, the LORD, a God merciful and gracious, slow to anger, and abounding in steadfast love and faithfulness."' We can take note of the context in which God says these words. Previously, in Exodus 20, God had given to Moses the Ten Commandments. These 10 laws were intended to form the basis of the Israelites' life together. However, within a short while, the people had turned away from God. They didn't fully trust that God alone could be their God. They weren't sure that God could look after them, keep them safe, and give prosperity and a future. As you can imagine things weren't looking good for their ongoing relationship with God. We might imagine that that would be the end of things.

But God and Moses have a conversation *(see Exodus 33. 12-23)* where they agree that they will have another go. And God promises to reveal himself to Moses, to show to Moses God's true and trustworthy nature. And it is here that we see God, not as angry and unforgiving, but as merciful, kind, and compassionate. And of course, this is not a one-off revelation of the nature of God. This description of God, compassionate and merciful, is often repeated.

The reality that 'God is love' is of course relevant for the entirety of creation. God creates all things in love: animal, vegetable, and mineral. God's love for all creation can be reflected in our relationship with all things.

The Apostle John reflects this awareness of the nature of God as the basis of the Christian faith. But he also reflects more personal and communal knowledge of the nature of God. John and all those believers circled around him reflect an awareness of the character and teaching of the Lord Jesus Christ.

In John's Gospel we are given a wonderful insight into the way in which we are to treat and serve one another and all else.

John has already described Jesus as being integral to God's act of creation *(see John 1. 1-3)*. When we read the words of John 13, we can therefore reflect on the idea that the loving Creator of all things kneels before the disciples to wash their feet. It is an act of extreme humility; and it reveals to us how love should work.

Love is humble. Love prefers to serve than to insist on power, status, and privilege. Love is kind, gentle, and yet is resolute for justice.

Group study material

"The love of God for humanity recalls Christians to the covenant relationship of grace and mercy in which God holds the Church and the world."

Discussion

A covenant is a 'deal' or binding agreement between two or more parties who are faithful to each other. Several covenants based on God's initiative are mentioned in the Bible – for example, with Noah, Abraham, Moses, David and the New Covenant in Christ *(see Jeremiah 31; 1 Corinthians 11. 25; Hebrews 8. 6-13)*.

- Can you think of stories from the Bible that show how loving God is?
- Can you recall from your own experience or the stories of others an example of the faithfulness, grace or mercy of God?
- When we talk of having a loving "relationship" with God, how would you describe that to a person with no previous knowledge of the Bible or Christianity?

"As churches that confess their faith in one God, Father, Son and Holy Spirit, and conscious of the special relationship with one another in Christ,
- * *we give thanks for all we have in common;*
- * *we acknowledge the richness of our diversity;*
- * *we are ashamed of the continuing consequences of division;*
- * *we share our understanding of the obedience to which we are called."*

- What would you say all Christian communities have in common in addition to their faith?
- How would you describe the "special relationship" between the churches of this area? (be honest and realistic)
- In what ways would you say the churches are "diverse"? (within themselves and between them all)
- What aspects of our divisions are we ashamed of?
- How would you describe "the obedience to which we are called"?
- What would you like to see improved in our relationships? How can that be done?

Please report your conclusions to the Churches Together Enabling Group.

Prayer suggestions

*In the shadow of your wings,
I will sing your praises, O Lord.*

The Lord is my light, my salvation; whom shall I fear?
The Lord is the refuge of my life; of whom shall I be afraid?

*In the shadow of your wings,
I will sing your praises, O Lord.*

One thing I ask of the Lord, one thing I seek;
to dwell in the presence of my God, to gaze on your holy place.

*In the shadow of your wings,
I will sing your praises, O Lord.*

I believe I shall see the goodness of the Lord in the land of the living.
O wait for the Lord! Have courage and wait, wait for the Lord.

*In the shadow of your wings,
I will sing your praises, O Lord.*

Christ be with me,
Christ within me,
Christ behind me,
Christ before me,
Christ beside me,
Christ to win me,
Christ to comfort me and restore me,
Christ beneath me,
Christ above me,
Christ in the hearts of all that love me,
Christ in mouth of friend and stranger.
In the Name of the Triune God,
Father, Son, and Holy Spirit.
Amen.   *From St Patrick's 'Breastplate'*

Circle me Lord
Keep protection near and danger afar.

Circle me Lord
Keep hope within
Keep doubt without.

Circle me Lord
Keep light near
And darkness afar.

Circle me Lord
Keep peace within
Keep evil out.

The Eternal Father encircle me
This day and always .
Amen. *David Adam*

- Pray for a fresh awareness that God is love.
- Praise God for all that Christians of different traditions have in common.
- Give thanks for the richness of our diversity in thinking, praying and worshipping.
- Repent of the divisiveness which brings dishonour to God and tarnishes our witness to his love.
- Pray for this group to be obedient to the call of the one Lord, Jesus Christ.

2 Making Jesus Christ known

Our Covenant commitment to God and one another

a We recognise in one another the same faith in Jesus Christ revealed in the Holy Scriptures, which the creeds of the ancient Church and other historic confessions seek to safeguard. We recognise in one another the same desire to hold this faith and proclaim the gospel in all its fullness.

b We intend so to act, speak and serve together in obedience to our Lord that the gospel of Jesus might be made known to others through the witness of our words, our lives and our faithfulness to Christ.

The Covenant Prayer

Loving Lord God,
we give you thanks for calling us together.
Guide us today
that in common obedience to our Lord Jesus Christ
and by the power of your Holy Spirit
we may learn together to serve you more faithfully
and search for the coming of your kingdom.
Amen.

Bible readings

John 2. 40-42 (NRSV)

One of the two who heard John speak ['There is the Lamb of God'] and followed him was Andrew, Simon Peter's brother. [41]He first found his brother Simon and said to him, "We have found the Messiah" (which is translated Anointed). [42]He brought Simon to Jesus, who looked at him and said, "You are Simon son of John. You are to be called Cephas" (which is translated Peter).

Acts 3. 1-10 *(NRSV)*

One day Peter and John were going up to the temple at the hour of prayer, at three o'clock in the afternoon. [2] *And a man lame from birth was being carried in. People would lay him daily at the gate of the temple called the Beautiful Gate so that he could ask for alms from those entering the temple.* [3] *When he saw Peter and John about to go into the temple, he asked them for alms.* [4] *Peter looked intently at him, as did John, and said, "Look at us."* [5] *And he fixed his attention on them, expecting to receive something from them.* [6] *But Peter said, "I have no silver or gold, but what I have I give you; in the name of Jesus Christ of Nazareth, stand up and walk."* [7] *And he took him by the right hand and raised him up; and immediately his feet and ankles were made strong.* [8] *Jumping up, he stood and began to walk, and he entered the temple with them, walking and leaping and praising God.* [9] *All the people saw him walking and praising God,* [10] *and they recognized him as the one who used to sit and ask for alms at the Beautiful Gate of the temple; and they were filled with wonder and amazement at what had happened to him.*

Sermon outline / Introduction

In the reading from John's Gospel we see …
1. Andrew was in relationship with his brother; he knew where he'd be and how to break the good news that had been foretold. The need for establishing a relationship before sharing the good news is important. Belonging frequently comes before belief.
2. We cannot give away what we haven't got: our own relationship with Christ is the basis of our making him known.
3. Great things can happen when a person follows Jesus. For instance, Andrew had a significant role in the of feeding the 5,000 *(see John 6. 1—15)*, and both Andrew and Peter went on to perform great works and to make Jesus known.

In the passage from Acts Peter and John make Christ known through action, speaking, and serving.
4. The severely lame man was simply asking for money; he must have been surprised that Peter and John demanded his attention, especially when Peter announced that the Apostles were broke!

Don't assume that Jesus' salvation and healing come only to people who are spiritually prepared or even religious. The gospel can come as a surprise.

5. Peter orders the man to do what he has never done before: *"stand up and walk!"*. This is not mind-over-matter or even 'faith healing', it is salvation (the word also means 'healing') *"in the name of Jesus Christ of Nazareth"*. It is the gospel in action and is the work of Jesus.

6. The result was extraordinary both in the case of the man who followed the Apostles to the Temple *"walking and leaping and praising God"*; and also in the effect - *"wonder and amazement"* – that this healing had on the people.

Making Jesus Christ known is first and foremost about consistent witness, living in way that commends him; it's what some have called 'making Christ visible'. Often it may take many years of patient witness before someone plucks up the courage to ask you about your faith.

Jesus Christ is also made known through evangelism, the public proclamation of the gospel by someone gifted for that ministry or by public acts by the churches together.

Whenever the good news is shared, practical signs of Jesus' presence are present – in the quality of our lives, and in healing, reconciliation, justice, and peace.

Group study material

"We recognise in one another the same faith in Jesus Christ revealed in the Holy Scriptures, which the creeds of the ancient Church and other historic confessions seek to safeguard. We recognise in one another the same desire to hold this faith and proclaim the gospel in all its fullness."

Discussion

- Can you give examples of when you have seen those of other Christians traditions than your own live out and exercise their faith?

- How do we make Christ known locally through our different traditions?
- How is our faithfulness to the good news seen and heard in this community and worldwide?
- Why are we sometimes hesitant to make Christ known?

"We intend so to act, speak and serve together in obedience to our Lord that the gospel of Jesus might be made known to others through the witness of our words, our lives and our faithfulness to Christ."

- What **actions** make Christ known locally?
- What **words** have we used or what words can we use to make Christ known?
- What **service** has resulted?
- In the light of our discussion what one thing could we actually do individually and collectively to make Christ known in this local area?
- What resources would we need?

Please report your conclusions to the Churches Together Enabling Group.

Prayer suggestions

God, our Father, we pray that through the Holy Spirit
we might hear your call to live as missionary disciples of your Son, Jesus.
Come Holy Spirit, fill the hearts of your faithful people
and renew us with the fire of your love.
May our communities always be places of joy and hope
that welcome the stranger and search for the lost.
We ask all this through Jesus Christ our Lord.
Amen.

- Give thanks for two millenia of the Church's witness to the Lord Jesus Christ.
- Praise God for the Scriptures of the Old and New Testaments.
- Pray for the strengthening of our actions, words and service together.
- Pray for obedience to the command to make Jesus known.
- Pray for wisdom in the way Churches Together engages in evangelism in our communities.
- Pray for our own faithful witness in word and action.

3 Serving human need

Our Covenant commitment to God and one another

a   We recognise in one another a shared awareness of God's call to serve his gracious purpose for all humanity.
b   We intend to work together for the freedom to flourish for all humanity, for justice and peace, for the healing of creation, and for the spiritual well-being of all.

The Covenant Prayer

Loving Lord God,
we give you thanks for calling us together.
Guide us today
that in common obedience to our Lord Jesus Christ
and by the power of your Holy Spirit
we may learn together to serve you more faithfully
and search for the coming of your kingdom.
Amen.

Bible reading

Matthew 9. 27-38 (REB)

[27] As he went on from there Jesus was followed by two blind men, shouting, 'Have pity on us, Son of David!' [28] When he had gone indoors they came to him, and Jesus asked, 'Do you believe that I have the power to do what you want?' 'We do,' they said. [29] Then he touched their eyes, and said, 'As you have believed, so let it be'; [30] and their sight was restored. Jesus said to them sternly, 'See that no one hears about this.' [31] But as soon as they had gone out they talked about him all over the region.

[32] *They were on their way out when a man was brought to him, who was dumb and possessed by a demon;* [33] *the demon was driven out and the dumb man spoke. The crowd was astonished and said, 'Nothing like this has ever been seen in Israel.'*
[35] *So Jesus went round all the towns and villages teaching in their synagogues, proclaiming the good news of the kingdom, and curing every kind of illness and infirmity.* [36] *The sight of the crowds moved him to pity: they were like sheep without a shepherd, harassed and helpless.* [37] *Then he said to his disciples, 'The crop is heavy, but the labourers too few;* [38] *you must ask the owner to send labourers to bring in the harvest.'*

Sermon outline / Introduction

1. This is one example of Jesus showing pity and compassion to people in human, physical need: in this case, blindness and possession which led to an inability to speak. There are many such passages in the Gospels, *(see for instance the healings in Mark 7. 24-37; Luke 4. 31-41; John 4. 43-54).*

2. Jesus is moved with compassion and describes the crowd as *"sheep without a shepherd"*, a common Old Testament simile *(see Numbers 27; 1 Kings 22; 2 Chronicles 18; Isaiah 13; Ezekiel 34, etc.).* Jesus also used the analogy of a lost sheep in parables he told about human lostness and God's compassion *(see Luke 15 and John 10. 1-16).* What could this could mean for us today? In what senses are we like a lost sheep or a flock of sheep without a shepherd?

3. Jesus still looks with compassion on a world which is lost and in need of healing, wholeness, and peace. In a practical sense, we are now the hands and feet of Jesus:
"Christ has no body now but yours. No hands, no feet on earth but yours. Yours are the eyes through which he looks with compassion on this world. Yours are the feet with which he walks to do good. Yours are the hands through

which he blesses all the world. Yours are the hands, yours are the feet, yours are the eyes, you are his body. Christ has no body now on earth but yours."*

Teresa of Avila was making the point that, for Christians, there is no choice about whether or not to serve human need: it is a fundamental part of our calling to be Christ's disciples.

4. Jesus speaks of the need for "*labourers to bring in the harvest*" (see Matthew 9. 37, 38; Luke 10. 1, 2). Who might these be? Could they be every one of us, individually and collectively, called to living and acting with compassion in our communities and across the world? You will know of examples of such willing service, locally and in the wider world, such as …

5. Some are called to the more obvious and visible aspects of serving human need but, for most of us, it is about turning the other cheek, giving away your coat, going the extra mile, loving and praying for your enemies *(see Matthew 5. 38-48)*, to show the love and compassion of Jesus in a needy world.

Group study material

"We recognise in one another a shared awareness of God's call to serve his gracious purpose for all humanity."

Discussion

- Can you describe an occasion when you lost something or someone, or you got lost, and how that made you feel at the time?

---

* *Words attributed to Teresa of Avila, 1515-82, a Spanish Carmelite nun who was a mystic and author of spiritual writings and poems. She founded numerous convents throughout Spain and initiated the reforms that restored a contemplative and austere life to the Carmelite order.*

- There are many examples in the Gospels of Jesus showing compassion for human need. Thinking of any of these stories, do any of them particularly speak to you? Can you explain why?
- What strikes you when you hear the words of Teresa of Avila?
- Can you recall a time when you have experienced God's blessing through other people?
- Harvest labourers work as a team. What are the advantages of team-working? Have you worked in a team whose members are from different Christian traditions?
- Were you aware of any long-term changes (in yourself and others) as a result of working in a cross-denominational team?

"We intend to work together for the freedom to flourish for all humanity, for justice and peace, for the healing of creation, and for the spiritual well-being of all."

- What examples can you give of people serving Christ to bring "freedom to flourish for all" in this locality or elsewhere?
- Can you think of any examples of Christians who have worked for justice and peace?

- What do you think is meant by the term "healing of creation"? How can you play a part in that?
- What other possibilities do we see for working together to serve human need in this community? – and in other places worldwide?
- Reflect quietly on James 2. 14-17 and then briefly share your thoughts about the link between physical and spiritual well-being.
  "What good is it, my friends, for someone to say he has faith when his actions do nothing to show it? Can that faith save him? [15] Suppose a fellow-Christian, whether man or woman, is in rags with not enough food for the day, [16] and one of you says, 'Goodbye, keep warm, and have a good meal,' but does nothing to supply their bodily needs, what good is that? [17] So with faith; if it does not lead to action, it is by itself a lifeless thing." (REB)

Please report your conclusions to the Churches Together Enabling Group.

Prayer suggestions

Heavenly Father, thank you that we are part of the body of Christ
and for the gifts and graces that you have given to each of us.
We pray that we may live our lives
according to your perfect plan and purposes.
Use us to compliment the work
carried out by our brothers and sisters in Christ,
and we pray that we may be a beautiful testimony
of the goodness and grace of Jesus Christ our Lord
to a lost and dying world.
Unite the whole body of Christ, with a dependant mutuality,
so that as individuals we may be truly united as one body,
to serve you in the place where you have planted us.
This we ask in Jesus' name.
Amen.
Adapted from: https://prayer.knowing-jesus.com/1-Corinthians/12/12

- Pray for our part in enabling all humans to flourish freely.
- Pray for peace in the world, not only the absence of aggression, but also reconciliation between people and nations.
- Pray for justice, truth, honesty, and integrity in national and international life, and for all who suffer injustice anywhere in the world.
- Pray for those persecuted for their faith, particularly for our Christian sisters and brothers.
- Pray for the spiritual well-being of all Jesus' disciples.
- Pray for the healing of creation, for the climate crisis, for future generations, and for the will to change our own behaviour for the better.

4 Being one body

Our Covenant commitment to God and one another

a We recognise one another as members of the Church of Jesus Christ, sharing in the unity of the Holy Spirit and committed to work for the coming of his Kingdom.
b We intend by the help of the Spirit to overcome those divisions which impede God's mission, obscure the gospel, and impair our witness. We intend to manifest our unity in Christ, that the world may believe.

The Covenant Prayer

Loving Lord God,
we give you thanks for calling us together.
Guide us today
that in common obedience to our Lord Jesus Christ
and by the power of your Holy Spirit
we may learn together to serve you more faithfully
and search for the coming of your kingdom.
Amen.

Bible reading 1 *Purity*

Mark 11. 15-19 (NRSV)

Then they came to Jerusalem. And he entered the temple and began to drive out those who were selling and those who were buying in the temple, and he overturned the tables of the money changers and the seats of those who sold doves; [16] and he would not allow anyone to carry anything through the temple. [17] He was teaching and saying, "Is it not written,
My house shall be called a house of prayer for all the nations'?
But you have made it a den of robbers."
[18] And when the chief priests and the scribes heard it, they kept looking for a way to kill him; for they were afraid of him, because the whole crowd was spellbound by his teaching. [19] And when evening came, Jesus and his disciples went out of the city.

Sermon outline 1 / Introduction 1

Jesus himself had ideas of what was holy and what needed to be defended. The coins of Empire carried the image of Caesar [the Emperor] as divine. You could not make an offering in the Temple of Israel's God with a coin claiming an alternative divinity. It was keeping the Temple of God pure that led to the existence of money-changers. Turning an otherwise-worthy act into a means of gaining personal profit tainted the worship of God. (This may well have been the act which confirmed that Jesus was taking his body into a dangerous place.)

The body of Christ is a common motif for the Church in the epistles of the New Testament *(see Ephesians 1. 22-23; 2. 11-22; 3. 3-9; 4. 7-16; 1 Corinthians 12. 12, 13; Romans 12. 3-5; Colossians. 1. 24; etc.)*.

Two key ideas in particular point to the corporate activity of the Spirit of God:

1. Spirituality is *communal* in the Church, as in Israel. In the Hebrew Bible, the primary unit of God's purpose and mission is Israel. The twelve disciples in the Gospels represent Jesus' Kingdom-of-God movement inheriting the mantle of the twelve tribes of Israel.
2. The body's functioning depends upon, even requires, diversity *(see 1 Corinthians 12. 21)*.

In the Covenant commitment, the first conviction for this section is that "We recognise one another as members of the Church of Jesus Christ, sharing in the unity of the Holy Spirit and committed to work for the coming of his Kingdom."

This does not say that we all have to be in agreement all of the time. Just as, individually, we have different temperaments, gifts and histories, so our worshipping traditions and denominations come from particular pasts. We see our journeys in different ways.

The Covenant commitment is both to recognise one another and share in unity of purpose.

When we consider church communities other than our own we should reflect on the criteria for admission to our own fellowship. What does it mean *for us* to be transformed into the likeness of Christ, to walk in the Spirit?

> St Ethelred's Church
>
> Acting perfect in Church is like getting dressed-up for an X-ray

The things which we regard as holy are protected by codes of behaviour. About a third of the encounters of Jesus in the gospels relate to codes of behaviour: With whom do we associate? Who do we share table with?

So, what are the non-negotiable signs of transformation in our own faith community? Where is the line beyond which we feel tainted or compromised? There are very many examples of these signs in the Gospels *(e.g. Luke 5. 29-31)*.

It is important to note that Jesus was not against his followers being transformed and distinct, he challenged some of the particular inherited ways of asserting the distinctiveness of God's people.

Group study material 1

"We recognise one another as members of the Church of Jesus Christ, sharing in the unity of the Holy Spirit and committed to work for the coming of his Kingdom."

Discussion

To grow as an intentional ecumenical mission, it is important to be reflective and note the *'but'* in our *'Yes, but'* about our fellow Christians of other traditions.

- What difference does it make to be a Christian in your tradition? Give examples of how salvation has changed you.
- Name the things that would compromise your witness or taint your fellowship.
- How can we better worship and serve alongside those who hold Christian perspectives with which we profoundly disagree? What prevents us from doing so?
- What would we be prepared to die for? What were the martyrs of our own tradition prepared to die for?

- What does 'our type of Christian' look like? (This may not be about faith or doctrine, it may be race, class, education, and a number of other categories which shape our churches.)

Bible readings 2 *Holiness*

2 Corinthians 3. 17, 18 (NRSV)

Now the Lord is the Spirit, and where the Spirit of the Lord is, there is freedom. ¹⁸ And all of us, with unveiled faces, seeing the glory of the Lord as though reflected in a mirror, are being transformed into the same image from one degree of glory to another; for this comes from the Lord, the Spirit.

2 Corinthians 4. 6 (NRSV)

For it is the God who said, 'Let light shine out of darkness', who has shone in our hearts to give the light of the knowledge of the glory of God in the face of Jesus Christ.

Sermon outline 2 / Introduction 2

One of the difficulties any human gathering experiences is that it gets into a groove, things become entirely predictable. This is simply a product of being human; all churches do it, too. The problem comes when our idea of the God we worship gets into a groove. It may be about our own spirituality, or, worse, our spirituality can be shaped by asserting that we are *not* like another group or person. *(Luke 18. 9-14, is a useful warning against this.)*

If we come to regard ourselves as one body across denominations, what is our shared journey if not to holiness? The letters to the early churches are addresses to people who are holy *(see 1 Thessalonians 4. 7)*.

Holiness cannot be domesticated; it is unsettling and can be a dangerous place *(see Exodus 3. 5; 19. 10-12; Joshua 5. 15; Acts 7. 33, etc)*.

As one body in Christ, what is our agenda? At the Last Supper in John's gospel, Jesus is about to sanctify [make holy] his body by taking it to a dangerous place, and a place of desecration and disgrace, outside the city, outside of the comfortable groove-places of familiarity. He wills that his disciples should follow him on that road (*John 17. 17*).

Holiness is about pursuing a way of life that will unsettle us, in order to open up our view of the world. Baptism takes us under water into a place of death. Holiness for Christians is to follow Jesus into the places of baptismal death.

Group study material 2

Discussion

"We intend by the help of the Spirit to overcome those divisions which impede God's mission, obscure the gospel, and impair our witness. We intend to manifest our unity in Christ, that the world may believe."

- Where are the 'death' places in our community in which we should look for Jesus?
- If Jesus visited this community, where would we find him? Where would he stay? Why do you think that?
- What do you think are the marks of holiness and why do we seek it?
- How would you describe the holiness of the Son of God?
- How did the Apostles become holy? What qualities were transformed in them? What did they have to discard in order to travel lighter?
- Name those things that impede God's mission, obscure the gospel and impair our witness.
- In what practical ways does our unity need to be *seen* in order to demonstrate the value of following Jesus?
- Are we prepared to be surprised into new ways of seeing and being the body of Christ? If so, give an example of your being surprised. If not, why not?

Between meetings, seek out representatives of other church traditions, and discuss the qualities of their church which we warm to, and which make us pause and think? Try to get beyond dealing with caricatures and deal with people who live the faith, do things differently and may believe differently.

Please report your conclusions to the Churches Together Enabling Group.

Prayer suggestions

Draw your Church together, O God,
into one great company of disciples,
together following our Lord Jesus Christ
into every walk of life,
together serving him in his mission to the world,
and together witnessing to his love
on every continent and Island.
Amen. *A New Zealand Prayer Book*

Using John 17. 10-26 as a departure point, shape prayers which explore the difference between being *the same*, and being *one body*.

Lord, lover of humankind,
fill us with the love your Spirit gives.
May we live in a manner worthy of our calling;
make us witnesses of your truth to all
and help us to work to bring all believers together
in the unity of faith and the fellowship of peace.
Amen. *The Weekday Missal*

- Pray for honesty about our own prejudices.
- Pray for the will to overcome the divisions that get in the way of God's work among us.
- Pray for willingness to set aside any behaviour or tradition that may obscure the gospel.
- Repent of all that impairs our witness to Christ and pray for the renewing power of the Holy Spirit.
- Pray that the world may believe.

5 Exercising God's gifts

Our Covenant commitment to God and one another

a   We recognise in one another the same call to every believer to share in the service of the church to the world, just as Christ lived among us as a servant.

b   We intend to seek those forms of common life which will enable all Christians to use the gifts bestowed on them in the service of God.

The Covenant Prayer

Loving Lord God,
we give you thanks for calling us together.
Guide us today
that in common obedience to our Lord Jesus Christ
and by the power of your Holy Spirit
we may learn together to serve you more faithfully
and search for the coming of your kingdom.
Amen.

Bible readings

Isaiah 42. 1-4, 6, 7 (REB)

Here is my servant, whom I uphold, my chosen one, in whom I take delight!
I have put my spirit on him; he will establish justice among the nations.
[2] He will not shout or raise his voice, or make himself heard in the street.
[3] He will not break a crushed reed or snuff out a smouldering wick;
unfailingly he will establish justice.
[4] He will never falter or be crushed until he sets justice on earth,
while coasts and islands await his teaching. ...
[6] I the LORD have called you with righteous purpose and taken you by the hand;
I have formed you, and destined you to be a light for peoples,
a lamp for nations, [7] to open eyes that are blind,

to bring captives out of prison, out of the dungeon where they lie in darkness.

Isaiah 50. 4-8a *(REB)*

The Lord God has given me the tongue of one who has been instructed to console the weary with a timely word;
he made my hearing sharp every morning, that I might listen like one under instruction.
⁵ The Lord God opened my ears and I did not disobey or turn back in defiance.
⁶ I offered my back to the lash, and let my beard be plucked from my chin,
I did not hide my face from insult and spitting.
⁷ But the Lord God is my helper; therefore no insult can wound me; I know that I shall not be put to shame, therefore I have set my face like flint.
⁸ One who will clear my name is at my side.

Sermon outline / Introduction

1. In the second part of the prophecies of Isaiah, written several centuries before Christ, there are four 'Servant Songs' *(Isaiah 42. 1-4; 49. 1-6; 50. 4-11; 52.13 – 53.12)*. They describe the Servant of the Lord, who may, originally, have been the prophet himself or a personification of God's people. The first Christians, having witnessed the Lord's miracles of healing *('to open eyes that are blind')*, and the humility of his passion and death *('I offered my back to the lash')*, came to identify Jesus, the Son and Servant of God, with these songs, and we continue to do so today.

2. As disciples of the Lord, we are called by him to a life of humble service, as he said, 'The greatest among you must be your servant.' *(Matthew 23. 11, 12; see also Luke 22. 24-29)* From the earliest days of

the Church, Christians have sought to love the Lord and our neighbours in lives of loving service: to God, to a broken world, and to our brothers and sisters in Christ *(see Matthew 5. 43-47; 22. 34-40; etc.)*. Of this there are many examples in the New Testament *(see, for instance, Acts 3. 2-10)*.

3. God bestows gifts on all for the common good. As Christians, we recognise and pray for the rich gifts and fruit of the Holy Spirit in our lives to enable us to worship and serve the Lord and his world. Jesus is the One who baptizes with the Holy Spirit *(see Matthew 3. 11)*. In John's Gospel, while preparing his disciples for his death *(see 14. 15-25; 15.26 – 16.15)*, Jesus tells them he will not leave them as orphans but send the Paraclete (Advocate, Counsellor, Helper - the Holy Spirit), not just to give us a better relationship with the Father and the Son but to fill us with power to be Christ's witnesses *(see Acts 1. 5, 8)*.

4. We don't have the original letter that the Corinthian Christians wrote to the Apostle Paul but they must have mentioned gifts from the Holy Spirit because he responds in 1 Corinthians 12-14. He begins by saying that the first sign of the Spirit's leading is to confess 'Jesus is Lord.' At a time when the Emperor and other 'gods' claimed to be 'Lord', this confession was the earliest Christian creed. Confessing 'Jesus is Lord' led many to a martyr's death.

5. Paul continues to describe the immense variety of the Holy Spirit's work: different gifts from one Spirit; different ways of serving one Lord; different abilities in each person but one God is served. The Spirit works uniquely in *each* of us "*for the good of all*". Every Christian, without exception, is called to desire and pray for the gifts and filling of the Spirit of God.

6. In these chapters Paul lists gifts and callings of the Spirit: wisdom, messages of knowledge, special faith, gifts of healing, miraculous powers, prophecy, being able to distinguish between spirits, speaking in tongues, and interpreting tongues. In Romans 12. 6-11, he supplements this list with the gifts of God: inspired speech, administration, counselling, giving, leading, helping. In both letters, he makes it clear that above all is the way of love. And in Ephesians 4. 11-13, we read of the gifts of the ascended Christ to apostles, prophets, evangelists, pastors and teachers, those who equip God's people and those who serve – all to build up the body of Christ and lead us all to *"the full stature of Christ"*.

7. The gifts and fruit of the Holy Spirit are many and varied – the list doesn't end *(see Galatians 5. 22-26; Philippians 4. 5-8)*. The Spirit's gifts are bestowed uniquely on every believer so that the command to love the Lord our God and our neighbours as ourselves *(see Matthew 22. 34-40; Mark 12. 28-31; Luke 10. 25-28)* can be fulfilled, not only by us as individuals but together as one body in Christ.

Group study material

"We recognise in one another the same call to every believer to share in the service of the church to the world, just as Christ lived among us as a servant."

Discussion
- What do we mean when we call Christ a 'servant'?
- In what ways are we servants?
- Whom do we serve?
- Non-Christians also serve. Can you give examples of serving alongside them?

- When we plan an act or venture of Christian service, how do we go about involving the faithful of other Christian traditions? If we don't, why not?

"We intend to seek those forms of common life which will enable all Christians to use the gifts bestowed on them in the service of God."

- As we have heard, Father, Son, and Holy Spirit all bestow gifts. What gifts do you recognise in yourself? – and in other Christians?
- What gifts can you think of in addition to those mentioned by Paul?
- What gifts do you covet – and why? (be as open as you can)
- Paul explains that the Spirit distributes different gifts to each person. Why is variety important for the body of Christ, his Church?
- The Apostle tells us that the Spirit's gifts are granted for the common good; how might his gifts be used for the good of all?
- How does using the gifts of the Spirit strengthen our united witness to Christ?
- Does your congregation have a particular God-given strength in any area? Could this be shared?
- Does your congregation have a particular weakness in any area? Could another church share gifts in order to help? How might that work?
- Share with each other what you experience of the work of the Holy Spirit in your life. Have you had any experience of the gifts of the Spirit listed by Paul? How could these good experiences improve our unity? In a moment, turn this into prayer.

Please report your conclusions to the Churches Together Enabling Group.

Prayer suggestions

You may wish to form groups of two or three and pray for one another to be filled with the power of the Holy Spirit and to bear the Spirit's fruit. Or ask someone you trust (maybe your minister or church leader) at a later date to pray with you.

- Praise God for Jesus the Servant of the Lord.
- Pray that God will make clear his calling to us as his servants.
- Pray that opportunities will be found to serve together.
- Pray that God will equip us with the gifts we need to fulfil God's call.
- Pray that we may bear the fruit of the Spirit.

As we wait in silence,
fill us with your Spirit.

As we worship you in majesty,
fill us with your Spirit.

As we listen to your word,
fill us with your Spirit.

As we long to be refreshed,
fill us with your Spirit.

As we long to be renewed,
fill us with your Spirit.

As we long to be equipped,
fill us with your Spirit.

As we long to be empowered,
fill us with your Spirit.

As we long to be united,
fill us with your Spirit. Amen.

6 Stronger together

Our Covenant commitment to God and one another

a We recognise in our congregational lives and patterns of worship, marks of love, joy, peace and holiness which are among the fruits of the Spirit.

b We intend to listen to one another and to appreciate the life and treasures of our various traditions, in order that the riches entrusted to us in separation may build up the whole Church of Christ.

The Covenant Prayer

Loving Lord God,
we give you thanks for calling us together.
Guide us today
that in common obedience to our Lord Jesus Christ
and by the power of your Holy Spirit
we may learn together to serve you more faithfully
and search for the coming of your kingdom.
Amen.

Bible readings

1 Corinthians 1. 10-13, 17, 18 (REB)

[10] *I appeal to you, my friends, in the name of our Lord Jesus Christ: agree among yourselves, and avoid divisions; let there be complete unity of mind and thought.* [11] *My friends, it has been brought to my notice by Chloe's people that there are quarrels among you.* [12] *What I mean is this: each of you is saying, 'I am for Paul,' or 'I am for Apollos'; 'I am for Cephas,' or 'I am for Christ.'* [13] *Surely Christ has not been divided! Was it Paul who was crucified for you? Was it in Paul's name that you were baptized? …* [17] *Christ did not send me to baptize, but to proclaim the gospel; and to do it without recourse to the skills of rhetoric, lest the cross of Christ be robbed of its effect.* [18] *The message of the cross is sheer folly to those on the way to destruction, but to us, who are on the way to salvation, it is the power of God.*

Ephesians 2. 12-22 *(REB)*

You were ... separate from Christ, excluded from the community of Israel, strangers to God's covenants and the promise that goes with them. Yours was a world without hope and without God. [13] Once you were far off, but now in union with Christ Jesus you have been brought near through the shedding of Christ's blood. [14] For he is himself our peace. Gentiles and Jews, he has made the two one, and in his own body of flesh and blood has broken down the barrier of enmity which separated them; [15] for he annulled the law with its rules and regulations, so as to create out of the two a single new humanity in himself, thereby making peace. [16] This was his purpose, to reconcile the two in a single body to God through the cross, by which he killed the enmity. [17] So he came and proclaimed the good news: peace to you who were far off, and peace to those who were near; [18] for through him we both alike have access to the Father in the one Spirit. [19] Thus you are no longer aliens in a foreign land, but fellow-citizens with God's people, members of God's household. [20] You are built on the foundation of the apostles and prophets, with Christ Jesus himself as the corner-stone. [21] In him the whole building is bonded together and grows into a holy temple in the Lord. [22] In him you also are being built with all the others into a spiritual dwelling for God.

Sermon outline / Introduction

1. In the first reading, the Apostle Paul confronts division in the Christian community at Corinth, an important trading city in Greece. There were serious moral and spiritual divisions there, as his letters make clear. Apollos was the principal mission-leader in Corinth, and Cephas [Peter] was certainly an important figure in the Church.

2. The Ephesians passage reflects a different kind of division, between Jewish and non-Jewish [Gentile] Christians. This was probably the

most serious division in the early Church, symbolised by the missions of Paul, based among Gentiles at Antioch, and James, the Lord's brother, based among Jews in Jerusalem. The letter sets out the principle that, whatever religious and social barriers once existed between people, all are united in Christ through the shedding of his blood. We read that Christ himself is the peace who brings us together into one body; the old enmity is dead; all are now built into God's new temple.

3. Divisions between Christian traditions still exist and they are often the product of history and genuine spiritual experiences of God, so should not be lightly dismissed as unimportant. One that sometimes bothers people is the difference in thinking between those Christians who view sharing in Holy Communion as a means of strengthening unity and other Christians who see this as the goal and sign of unity.

Our covenant does not shy away from important matters that divide Christian denominations, including differences in the way we worship God, but it draws our attention to far more important principles: love, joy, peace, and holiness. ("Peace" is an ancient word, found in Hebrew and many other languages, meaning God's gift of the freedom to flourish.) These are the fruit of the Holy Spirit's work, and they unite Christians. Paul describes them in Galatians chapter 5:

"... [22] *the fruit of the Spirit is love, joy, peace, patience, kindness, goodness, faithfulness,* [23] *humility and self-control. ...* [25] *If the Spirit is the source of our life, let the Spirit also direct its course.*

4. We have much to learn from one another, if we pause and listen to what others are saying, and see what they are doing, in order to learn from them and share with them. Too often a genuine thankfulness for our local fellowship can turn into pride, that assumes no one else can help us. Yet, each part of the Body of Christ has treasures to share with others, and weaknesses in which they can be supported by others – if only we would allow them.

The Covenant lifts our eyes beyond our local congregation, beyond our tradition, beyond our 'western' way of being Church, to the fruit of the Holy Spirit: love, joy, peace, and holiness. The Covenant rejects introversion, which is why it does not focus on these principles simply to make us comfortable and content as we are, but to make us useful for God. We're called to make a difference together, and the marks of togetherness are love, joy, peace and holiness.

Group study material

"We recognise in our congregational lives and patterns of worship, marks of love, joy, peace and holiness which are among the fruits of the Spirit."

Discussion

- Thinking of your own congregation, can you give examples of the marks of love, joy, peace, and holiness?
- And can you think of times when these marks were missing?
- Do any of the divisions between the churches bother you? Why? Or why not?
- Stage a mini debate between those who say that the divisions within or between the churches make nonsense of the gospel-message, and those who say divisions are not important.

"We intend to listen to one another and to appreciate the life and treasures of our various traditions, in order that the riches entrusted to us in separation may build up the whole Church of Christ."

- What would you say are the "treasures" of your own church tradition?
- Can you think of one thing you have learned from a Christian tradition other than your own?
- Are there any treasures of other church traditions that you would appreciate in your own?
- What's the best way to share these treasures? (don't say 'use the church leaders'!)
- In what practical ways can we grow stronger together?
- Should we be searching for a common meeting venue of some kind? (ideas, please)

Please report your conclusions to the Churches Together Enabling Group.

Prayer suggestions

Gracious Father,
we pray for those who, through the witness of the Apostles,
have put their faith in the Lord Jesus.
Let them all be one;
as you, Father, are in your Son, and he is in you,
so also may your people be in you,
that the world may believe that you sent Jesus.
The glory which you gave him he has given to us,
that we may be one, as you and your Son are one;
Christ in us and you in him, may we be perfectly one,
that the world will know that you sent him,
and that you love us as you loved him.
Father, your people are your gift to your Son;
and his desire is that we may be with him where he is,
so that we may look upon his glory, which you have given him
because you loved him before the world began.
Righteous Father, although the world does not know you,
the Lord Jesus knows you,
and your people know that you sent him.
He made your name known to us, and will make it known,
so that the love you had for your Son may be in us,
and he may be in all your people.
Amen.　　　　　　　　　　　　　　　*Based on John 17. 20-26*

- Give thanks for God's treasures in our various Christian communities.
- Give thanks for the fruit of the Spirit in our churches.
- Pray for the free sharing of God's gifts among the churches.
- Pray for a willingness to look at, listen to and learn from others.

Holy Spirit of God, unite us in the love of Jesus and make us stronger together to serve your world. **Amen.**

7 The way forward

This study should take place ecumenically, whenever possible

Our final Covenant commitment to God and one another

In faithfulness to the Word of God we believe that God will guide his Church into ways of truth and peace, correcting and healing, strengthening and renewing according to the mind of Christ. We approach the future with openness to the Holy Spirit.

We therefore urge the people of all our churches to love one another in the Holy Spirit as God loves the world, and to take every opportunity to grow together in Christ through common prayer and worship, mutual listening, understanding, action and love, that we may be renewed together for mission.

We are committed before God and with one another to the Covenant for Mission: to work and pray in common obedience to our Lord Jesus Christ, that by the power of the Holy Spirit we may serve together in Evesham and District for the coming of the Kingdom and to the glory of God the Father.

The Covenant Prayer

> Loving Lord God,
> we give you thanks for calling us together.
> Guide us today
> that in common obedience
>   to our Lord Jesus Christ
> and by the power of your Holy Spirit
> we may learn together
>   to serve you more faithfully
> and search for the coming of your kingdom.
> **Amen.**

Bible readings

John 13. 34, 35 (REB)

Jesus said: ^{34}*'I give you a new commandment: love one another; as I have loved you, so you are to love one another.* ^{35}*If there is this love among you, then everyone will know that you are my disciples.' ...*

John 15. 7-17 (REB)

'If you dwell in me, and my words dwell in you, ask whatever you want, and you shall have it. ^{8}*This is how my Father is glorified: you are to bear fruit in plenty and so be my disciples.* ^{9}*As the Father has loved me, so I have loved you. Dwell in my love.* ^{10}*If you heed my commands, you will dwell in my love, as I have heeded my Father's commands and dwell in his love.* ^{11}*'I have spoken thus to you, so that my joy may be in you, and your joy complete.* ^{12}*This is my commandment: love one another, as I have loved you.* ^{13}*There is no greater love than this, that someone should lay down his life for his friends.* ^{14}*You are my friends, if you do what I command you.* ^{15}*No longer do I call you servants, for a servant does not know what his master is about. I have called you friends, because I have disclosed to you everything that I heard from my Father.* ^{16}*You did not choose me: I chose you. I appointed you to go on and bear fruit, fruit that will last; so that the Father may give you whatever you ask in my name.* ^{17}*This is my commandment to you: love one another.'*

Sermon outline / Introduction

1. 'What good would it do me to be a Christian disciple? You're divided into so many denominations; you have different buildings, different doctrines, different forms of worship and ministry; even worse, that seems to be the way most of you like it. Now you suggest that I should become a disciple! Why on earth would I do that?' It's a fair point.

2. We've reached the conclusion of our seven studies/sermons on the Covenant for Mission. We hope you are committed to the vision of God's mission in unity in five key areas:
   Making Jesus Christ known
   Serving human need
   Being one body
   Exercising God's gifts
   Stronger together
3. We were reminded in the first study/sermon that love – for God and for others – is at the heart of our Christian obedience. In this last session we begin a search for the way forward. The final three paragraphs of the Covenant commit us …
   to look for God's guidance,
   to deepen our love, and
   to work and pray for the coming of God's Kingdom.

4. Jesus says, *"I am the vine;"* it's the last of his *"I am"* sayings in John's Gospel, Not "I am **like** a vine," but, *"I am the vine,"* - the Lord united with the Father and with his people. We *"dwell"* in him, he *"remains"* in us and he is our *"friend".* Our Lord gives us, his disciples, three vital commands: to dwell in his love; to love one another; and to bear fruit plentifully. Thus we will be known as his disciples.

5. In order to fulfil these commands, we need to be open to the guidance of the Holy Spirit (*see John 15. 26, 27 and Galatians 5. 22-25*), and to make our commitment with the utmost seriousness (*see Philippians 1. 9-11*).

Group study material

"In faithfulness to the Word of God we believe that God will guide his Church into ways of truth and peace, correcting and healing, strengthening and renewing according to the mind of Christ. We approach the future with openness to the Holy Spirit.

"We therefore urge the people of all our churches to love one another in the Holy Spirit as God loves the world, and to take every opportunity to grow together in Christ through common prayer and worship, mutual listening, understanding, action and love, that we may be renewed together for mission.

"We are committed before God and with one another to the Covenant for Mission: to work and pray in common obedience to our Lord Jesus Christ, that by the power of the Holy Spirit we may serve together in Evesham and District for the coming of the Kingdom and to the glory of God the Father."

Discussion

- When you're confused about the future, what do you do? (be honest).
- If you'd been a first century Christian disciple, which of the characters in the New Testament would you have found it difficult to get along with – and why?
- Did Jesus always get along well with his friends? Can you remember times when they irritated or offended him? (*if stuck, see Mark 3. 5; 10. 14*)
- What do you think other people find irritating about you?
- Which, on balance, would you say most encourages people to become Christian disciples: teaching or example? Share why you think as you do.

What do we intend to do?

- What one suggestion can you make to help us seek God's guidance, for you as an individual? And for the Christian communities of this locality?
- Where do you usually look when you are searching for the Kingdom? Where else could you look?
- What one proposal would deepen the love between Christians of different traditions here?
- Thinking about the whole course of sermons / studies, what one thing has made the greatest impact on you?

Please review and report your conclusions from all these studies to the Churches Together Enabling Group.

Prayer suggestions

Holy Spirit of God, guide us and deepen our love, as we look for the coming of the Kingdom; and surprise us all. **Amen.**

- Give thanks for what we have shared and learned in these studies.
- Give thanks for our common life in Christ across all traditions.
- Pray for openness to the Holy Spirit and one another.
- Pray for the coming of the Kingdom of God on earth as in heaven.
- Pray for the Covenant and its principles to become deeply embedded in the life of all the Christian communities here.

The leader reads 'Our Covenant commitment to God and one another' and we respond:

O Lord, in faithfulness to your Word, we believe that you will guide your Church into ways of truth and peace, correcting and healing, strengthening and renewing according to the mind of Christ. We approach the future with openness to the Holy Spirit.
Amen. Lord, begin with me.

We therefore pray that the people of all our churches will love one another in the Holy Spirit as you love the world, and will take every opportunity to grow together in Christ through common prayer and worship, mutual listening, understanding, action and love, that we may be renewed together for mission.
Amen. Lord, begin with me.

We are committed before you and with one another to the Covenant for Mission: to work and pray in common obedience to our Lord Jesus Christ, that by the power of the Holy Spirit we may serve together in this area for the coming of your Kingdom and to your glory, O God our Father.
Amen. Lord, begin with me.

Conclude by saying together:

**Now to him who is able
through the power which is at work among us
to do immeasurably more
   than all we can ask or conceive,
to him be glory in the church and in Christ Jesus
from generation to generation for ever!
Amen.**   *Ephesians 3. 20, 21*

Appendix

Additional material relevant to each chapter for optional use

1 The love of God

In a covenant, two or more individuals, each respecting the dignity and the integrity of the other, come together in a bond of love and trust, to share their interests, sometimes even to share their lives, by pledging our faithfulness to one another, to do together what neither of us can do alone.
And that is not the same as a contract at all. A contract is a *transaction*, but a covenant is a *relationship*. Or to put it slightly differently: a contract is about interests, but a covenant is about identity. And that is why contracts *benefit*, but covenants *transform*.
Chief Rabbi Jonathan Sacks, 2008

We must grow 'til our arms get right 'round the world.
General William Booth (1829-1912)

We come to God not by walking but by loving [*non ambulando, sed amando*]. We are carried to him not by our feet but by our moral character, and moral character is assessed not by what a person knows but by what a person loves.   *Augustine of Hippo (354-430): Epistles*

The only place where you can be safe from love is hell.
C. S. Lewis (1898-1963)

Leif Peterson said, at the funeral of his father, Eugene, that his dad had only one sermon and only one message, for all his books and years of ministry, words that he had said over Leif as he slept as a child and that whispered in his heart for 50 years: 'God loves you. God is on your side. He is coming after you. He is relentless.'

Thy nature and thy name is Love.
> *Line repeated several times in Charles Wesley's hymn, 'Wrestling Jacob'*

Many will recall the lilting voice of Desmond Tutu who, with a twinkle in his eye, told congregations around the world, 'All I have is one sermon . . . the incredible love of God for all people. God loves you. Final stop.' And with a belly laugh he added, 'God has remarkably low standards.'
Anglican and Episcopal History

Christians have often said that love is someone else's reality living in you. It's not just an attitude to someone or something. It changes you. Someone else is living in the 'house' of your mind and your feelings. That's why, when we talk about 'loving God' we don't just mean that we feel something about God. God has come to live in the house. Loving God is God's gift, God's action in us, not a thing we do, or a set of nice warm feelings about him. Real Christian love, then, is what the Bible calls 'communion', sharing life together. I love God through the 'communion of the Holy Spirit', God's breath breathing in my lungs, God living in my house. And if I learn what that means, I know why it is that real, grown-up love is the way it is. In all my relationships now, I've got to try and let that kind of love develop - letting other people live in me, letting my thoughts and feelings be changed by what they think I feel.
Rowan Williams, 2001

2 Making Jesus Christ known

Evangelization is the mission of the Church. Not just of a few, but my, your, our mission. Pope Francis

Romans 10. 13-15 ('How can they hear without someone to preach?')
How do you like that bird I sent you home for your birthday? ... You cooked it? ... Mamma, that was a South American parrot - he spoke five languages! ... He should have SAID something!
George Jessel: Phone Call to Mama

The life of Jesus spills out into the lives of those who receive him and then continues to spill out all over the place.
Eugene Peterson: The Message – Introduction to Philippians

Evangelism means to carry Jesus in your heart and to give the presence of Jesus to someone else. They see God in us and we also see God in them. But to give Jesus to a person, you must first have Jesus yourself.
Mother Theresa of Calcutta

I have lived much of my life in an immediate concern for the evangelisation of the world, and I have come to see that it is almost useless to nag at Christians, telling them they ought to witness to their faith. The gospel is not preached out of a sense of duty. It is overheard when people make a fresh discovery of the power of Christ and can't help talking about it. And that fresh discovery is usually made at the end of our tether.
John V. Taylor

If all the sons [and daughters] of the church could be untiring missionaries of the gospel, a new flowering of sanctity and of renewal would rise up in the world thirsting for love and truth.
Pope John Paul I (the '30-day Pope') immediately after his election

Unless the Church reaches out it passes out.
Anon.

Evangelism is one beggar telling another where to get bread. *D. T. Niles*

Don't let anyone talk the Church out of dialogue with non-Christians; this is evangelism and evangelism leads to conversion. Evangelism and proselytism are different from each other: proselytism takes the end-product and simply copies it. Conversion is a truly catholic event.
Fr Vincent J Donovan, 1997

It is inexcusable for an evangelist to make Christ sound boring, but some succeed in doing so.
Edward Patey: Open the Doors, 1978

An Alternative Parable of the Sower

A farmer once gave his labourer a bag of seed to sow on his field but as he went he began to reason with himself, 'It seems a shame to just throw this seed around! Some of it will certainly fall onto the path and those birds will get it, sure's eggs is eggs! I'll be careful and avoid the paths.'
Then, as he walked, he saw the rocky soil and he thought, 'It won't be much use sowing the seed here: it'll grow all right, but then it'll soon dry up and that will be the end of it. I'll make sure I don't waste seed on the rocky bits!'
As he plodded on with his basket, he came across a big patch of weeds, and murmured, 'It'll be no good sowing any seed near there, the suckers will soon come out and grow round the corn, and the good seed will have been wasted - I'll leave that bit.'
At last he reached some good soil and he thought he'd begin to sow - carefully, mind you, in case he upset the neighbours by throwing a handful of seed across their land - but it was time to go home.
'Ah well,' he thought, 'there'll be another time.'

Robert Paterson, 1990

3   Serving human need

Additional Bible passages to explore:
Matthew 14. 14 (Jesus' heart went out to the crowd);
    15. 32-39 (feeding the 4,000).
Mark 6 (several healings).
Luke 17. 11-19 (ten healed, one gave thanks).

The Church should consist of communities of loving defiance. Instead it consists largely of comfortable clubs of conformity.

Ronald J. Sider: Rich Christians in an Age of Hunger

The Church is called to walk in the world as Jesus walked the land. ... This wandering ecclesia [church] moves beyond the sanctuary in daily actions ... encounters occur within the boundaries of sacred places, in the context of intentional mission and engagement with the community, and in multiple contexts of human discourse and exchange.
Julie Gittoes, Where is the Kingdom? - in Generous Ecclesiology, 2013

I prefer a Church which is bruised, hurting and dirty because it has been out on the streets, rather than a Church which is unhealthy from being confined and from clinging to its own security. I do not want a Church concerned with being at the centre and which then ends by being caught up in a web of obsessions and procedures.
Pope Francis: The Joy of the Gospel, 2013

Holding the beggar's child
Against my heart
Through blinding tears, I see
That as I hold the tiny, piteous thing
So God loves me.   Dr Toyohiko Kagawa

As long as the problems of the poor are not radically resolved by rejecting the absolute autonomy of markets and financial speculation and by attacking the structural causes of inequality, no solution will be found for the world's problems or, for that matter, to any problems. Inequality is the root of social ills.
Pope Francis: The Joy of the Gospel, 2013

In another walk to Salisbury, he [George Herbert, poet and priest, 1593-1633] saw a poor man with a poorer horse that was fallen under his load; they were both in distress, and needed present help, which Mr. Herbert perceiving, put off his canonical coat, and helped the poor man to unload, and after to load his horse. The poor man blessed him for it, and he blessed the poor man; and was so like the good Samaritan, that he gave him money to refresh both himself and his horse, and told him that if he loved himself, he should be merciful to his beast. Thus he left the poor man, and at his coming to his musical friends at Salisbury, they began to wonder that Mr. George Herbert, who used to be so trim and

clean, came into that company so soiled and discomposed; but he told them the occasion; and when one of the company told him he had disparaged himself by so dirty an employment, his answer was, that the thought of what he had done would prove music to him at midnight, and that the omission of it, would have upbraided and made discord in his conscience, whensoever he would pass by that place. 'For if I be bound to pray for all that be in distress, I am sure that I am bound, so far as it is in my power, to practise what I pray for. And though I do not wish for the like occasion every day, yet let me tell you, I would not willingly pass one day of my life without comforting a sad soul, or showing mercy; and I praise God for the occasion. And now let's tune our instruments.'
Izaac Walton: The Life of Mr. George Herbert, 1670

4 Being one body

Christianity is a social religion. To turn it into a solitary religion is to destroy it.   *John Wesley*

If only I may grow firmer, simpler, quieter, warmer.
Dag Hammarskjold: Markings

The Christian religion isn't about being good, it is about being holy, and being holy has nothing to do with being pious. It has much more to do with becoming or being the person God created and wants us to be, of "growing up in every way, into him who is the head, into Christ" (Ephesians 4. 15).   *David Hope, 1989*

You see, the goal of the Christian life is not simply to get us into heaven, but to get heaven into us!   *Richard Foster: Streams of Living Water*

There can be no holiness, but social holiness.   *John Wesley (1703-91)*

The Church is not a bouquet of individuals.   *P.T. Forsyth (1848-1921)*

Holiness there [at the Last Supper] is seen as going into the heart of where it's most difficult for human beings to be human. Jesus goes *'outside the city';* he goes to the place where people suffer and are humiliated, the place where people throw stuff out, including other people. *'Outside the camp'*, in the language of the Old Testament *(see also Hebrews 13.13)*. If we take this seriously, the Christian idea of holiness is to do with going where it's most difficult, in the name of Jesus who went where it was most difficult. He wants us to be holy like that.

Rowan Williams: Being Disciples, 2016

… there are some Christians who spend their lives going from church to church on safari, looking for that rarest of species, perfectus churchimus. If they ever managed to find it, they'd render it extinct immediately by joining it. *Adrian Plass & Jeff Lucas: Seriously Funny*

Church is what happens when the impact of Jesus draws people together. *Rowan Williams, 2001*

5 Exercising God's gifts

Following on from 1 Corinthians 12, read chapters 13 & 14 and discuss how the advice Paul gives in all three chapters affects how we should exercise the Spirit's gifts.

It is easy to want things from the Lord and yet not want the Lord himself; as though the gift could ever be preferable to the Giver.

Augustine of Hippo (354-430)

The Church and the Christian alike are committed to service as the expression of the love and compassion of God in the name of Jesus Christ. Unless the Church is at home in the sphere of service, it is unlikely to be relevant when it turns to evangelism.

Douglas Webster: What is Evangelism?

Every time we say, 'I believe in the Holy Spirit,' we mean that we believe that there is a living God able and willing to enter human personality and change it.
J.B. Phillips

David Watson told his hearers that 'the aim of being filled with the Holy Spirit was not primarily that we may feel better but that God would make us more useful in his service.'   *David Armstrong: in David Watson, 1985*

The chief actor in the historic mission of the Christian Church is the Holy Spirit. He is the director of the whole enterprise. God's mission consists of the things he is doing in the world.   *John V Taylor*

Each one has a place in the Community of Christ, and ought to fill it, but he [and she] ought not to be everywhere and want to take part in everything. ... Take note of what God gives you, then you will also know the task he sets you.
Emil Brunner: The Letter to the Romans (on Romans 12. 3-8)

An act of commitment

Empowered by the Holy Spirit, will you dare to walk into God's future, trusting him to be your guide?
By the Spirit's power, we will.
Will you dare to embrace each other and grow together in love?
By the Spirit's power, we will.
Will you dare to share your riches and minister to each other in need?
By the Spirit's power, we will.
Will you dare to pray for each other until your hearts beat with the longings of God?
By the Spirit's power, we will.
Will you dare to carry the light of Christ into the world's dark places?
By the Spirit's power, we will.

6 Stronger together

The church exists to set up in the world a new sign which is radically dissimilar to the world's own manner and which contradicts it in a way which is full of promise.
Karl Barth, quoted in Philip Yancey's 'Church: Why Bother?'

In necessary things, unity; in doubtful things, liberty; in everything, charity. *Motto of Richard Baxter (1615-91)*

The Christian Church is not a club that we belong to in order that our needs might be met; it is a body, a building, a family, and army - these are some of the pictures used to show that, by accepting the call of Christ, we have responsibilities that we cannot avoid if we are to be his disciples. It is not a matter of our feelings and personal choices; it is a matter of taking with the utmost seriousness the conditions and demands of discipleship that Jesus lays upon us. We are no longer our own. We have been chosen by him, called by him, bought by him; we therefore now belong to him, and by virtue of this fact we also belong to one another, however easy or difficult, joyful or painful, we may find this to be. *David Watson: Discipleship, 1981*

[The Church] is a wonderful and most extra-ordinary pageant of contradiction, and I, at least, want to be inside it, though it is foolishness to most of my friends. *Rose Macaulay: The Towers of Trebizond, 1956*

We seem to have allowed the Church to be depicted as a sad and lifeless institution, with no interest in spiritual matters. Moreover, there is some evidence suggesting that the Church's justifiable concern with political and economic affairs has contributed to this understanding.
... The Christian message is often ignored today because the church projects itself as an institution that is bothered only about matters that to other people seem like trivialities.
John Drane: New Spiritualities and Christian Mission

7 The way forward

If Christians wish us to believe in their redeemer, why don't they look a little more redeemed?   *Friedrich Nietzche (1844-1900)*

The story is told of an Indian catechist at the end of the nineteenth century dismissed from the Church for some misdemeanour. Burdened with shame, knowing he would never again dare to preach, the man left the area and went to some far-off village where there was no Christian community at all. There, where he was completely unknown, where malicious Christian gossip could never reach him, he settled down and made his living as a potter. The Church never heard of him again and he died there. Years later it was decided to send a team of evangelists to that very place. They rented a house and began to tell the stories of Christ. They were amazed when the crowd of villagers responded eagerly, 'We know the man you are talking about! He lived here for years!' 'No,' said the preachers, 'you don't understand. We are talking about Jesus Christ.' 'Well,' answered the people, 'he never told us his name. But the man you describe is our potter without a doubt.'
     John V. Taylor: Man in the Midst, Highway, 1955

Of a truth, unity and concord doth best become religion; yet is not unity the sure and certain mark whereby we know the Church of God.
     John Jewel (1522 - 1571): Works, Vol III

[Communion amid disagreement] can only be achieved by those great persons who are willing to go beyond the surface of the conflict and to see others in their deepest dignity. This requires acknowledging a principle indispensable to the building of friendship in society: namely, that unity is greater than conflict.
     Pope Francis: The Joy of the Gospel, 2013